watching glory die

judith thompson
watching glory die

Playwrights Canada Press
Toronto

For professional or amateur production rights, please contact:
Rena Zimmerman, Great North Artists Management
350 Dupont Street, Toronto, ON M5R 1V9
416.925.2051, renazimmerman@gnaminc.com

LIBRARY AND ARCHIVES CANADA CATALOGUING IN PUBLICATION

Thompson, Judith, 1954-, author
Watching Glory die / Judith Thompson.

A play.
Issued in print and electronic formats.
ISBN 978-1-77091-515-2 (paperback).--ISBN 978-1-77091-516-9 (pdf).--
ISBN 978-1-77091-518-3 (mobi).--ISBN 978-1-77091-517-6 (epub)

I. Title.

PS8589.H4883W38 2016   C812.54   C2016-905699-6
                                               C2016-905700-3

We acknowledge the financial support of the Canada Council for the Arts, the Ontario Arts Council (OAC), the Ontario Media Development Corporation, and the Government of Canada through the Canada Book Fund for our publishing activities. Nous remercions l'appui financier du Conseil des Arts du Canada, le Conseil arts de l'Ontario (CAO), la Société de développement de l'industrie des médias de l'Ontario, et le Gouvernement du Canada par l'entremise du Fonds du livre du Canada pour nos activités d'édition.

Canada Council
for the Arts
Conseil des arts
du Canada

ONTARIO ARTS COUNCIL
CONSEIL DES ARTS DE L'ONTARIO
an Ontario government agency
un organisme du gouvernement de l'Ontario

Canada

Ontario
Ontario Media Development
Corporation

This is dedicated to Ashley Smith, and her mother, Coralee Smith.

The world premiere of *Watching Glory Die* was presented by Canadian Rep Theatre at Vancouver's The Cultch in April 2014 with the following cast and creative team:

Performed by Judith Thompson
Directed by Ken Gass and Nicky Guadagni
Stage management by Nan Shepherd
Set and costume design by Astrid Janson
Lighting design by André du Toit
Sound design by Debashis Sinha
Projection design by Cameron Davis

playwright's note

This play is inspired by the tragic death of nineteen-year-old Ashley Smith in her isolation cell at Grand Valley Institution for Women in 2007; Ashley had been in the Canadian correctional system since she was fourteen years old, and the system that destroyed her continues to destroy other Canadian women, particularly Indigenous women.

We must stop being bystanders.

characters

Glory
Rosellen
Gail

GLORY #1

GLORY is onstage, drawing with her finger on her cell walls, an elaborate scene. She is writing a poem.

GAIL #1

My brother James had a glass eye. From fallin' on a barbed wire fence when he was only six. He would pop it out, throw it in the air, and catch it in his mouth to scare people. Joker, eh? You woulda liked James. Everyone liked James—a big goofy smile for everyone, you know? So just like Dad, and myself, and our three sisters, James went into corrections as soon as he graduated the college corrections course. And he went in with exactly the right attitude: this is not social services, this is corrections. This is jail. These are the criminals, and we are what is keepin' them from . . . freedom. We are the screws . . . holdin' in the deadbolt. We are, basically, in a cold war.

But he did his job real well, highly regarded, on track for promotions. Got married to the lovely Nancy. They lived in this kinda shitty basement apartment in town, but they dreamed of a farm, outside the city. They talked about this all the time. And I mean ALL the time.

So you know that smile James always had on his face? He did not have it for the inmates, I never saw him smile at any of them once, until—this one day in winter . . . about ten years in . . . I seen him, smilin' like an idiot at this one inmate.

And talkin' to him, like a friend. Frequently.

I didn't say nothin', I figured it was none of my business. They would talk about hockey mainly. And women.

And then . . .

I don't know. I don't know how it happened. Maybe it was the farm dream, maybe it was this guy had some kinda like, spidey power. He was a con, right, but James should have been onto that. Maybe it was because he was sick of seeing others doin' it and getting rich off it—and not getting caught.

But one thing led to another, and soon—you guessed it—

James was . . . you know . . . bringin' in . . . contraband—and Nancy, she was right in there makin' up the condoms or whatever. I didn't know, of course I didn't, but in a kinda sideways way I knew. In that kinda way, everyone knew.

Soon Jamesy got in so deep he could not crawl out . . . On the one side, if my little brother didn't say "How high?" when the biker gangs said "Jump," he would be killed—straight up—and if he turned hisself in, well, if a CO does time, we all know what happens.

As my dad used to say, he didn't know whether to shit or go blind.

There was only one solution.

They lived on the farm, now, right?

That was the dream farm: they had a pond, they had three horses, they had the goats, deer, they grew corn.

One Sunday they make themselves a picnic—chicken salad sandwiches, roast turkey, potato salad, chocolate cake, two bottles of the best wine, and they ride their horses as far out on their property as they can. They let the horses go. They spread out their red checkered picnic blanket. They eat their picnic lunch. They drink all the wine. They put their arms around each other.

And they shoot each other in the back of the head.

I wonder, you know? If what happened to my brother Jamie— might have something to do with why I could not do . . . what I knew . . . was the . . . right . . . the only right . . .

ROSELLEN #1

I hate those apples now. I gaze out my window at those nasty crabapples every morning and I scold them; I say, "How is it that you are responsible for my beautiful daughter being locked up like an animal since she was fourteen years old, and young for fourteen, a baby really, and you are sitting there on that branch just happy? How is it? That a tiny little fruit could cause a catastrophe?"

Apparently, to toss an apple, to hit a mean-spirited postman in the back of the knees, is assault.

And she didn't exactly help herself.

Oh, Glory, you would have to pull the fire alarm in the police station after shoplifting a CD all because you were havin' so much fun in juvenile detention with your new friends, you wanted to go back, you finally fit in somewhere! But they didn't know that, nor did they care. Stealing is a crime and you were gonna pay for it and pay for it you have.

It has been *five years*. Oh yes. Oh YES, originally sentenced to six months, just six months in juvenile detention when she was fourteen! I tell people that, no one can believe it. She has never, ever been violent, or committed any crime, other than bein' a giant pain in the butt sometimes—but that six months has lasted for five years. You may be wondering how the hell does THAT happen?

Well I'll tell you.

Eight hundred incident reports.

Five hundred "institutional charges." And what do you think those charges were for? Swiping a pencil, telling a rough guard to eff off, maybe even spitting.

Oh you might be thinking but surely, surely she musta done something more serious to rack up all them charges, in this country even rapists get out after a year or two for good behaviour . . .

Listen to me: they film every single interaction with the inmates . . . They have everything, everything on film in order to protect themselves, right? Union rules. Do you think for a MINUTE, if

Glory had been violent, that they would not have caught that on film?

I asked them: I said, "do you have any of this on film?"

They wouldn't answer me. Because they know the charges are garbage. Lies.

They don't like her, because she doesn't say, "Yes sir no sir three bags full sir," because she is fearless. My Glory is fearless.

Oh yes. She woulda been a revolutionary, you see, in another time, another place. I could imagine Glory leading peasants through the jungle, fearless.

But now. Oh she puts on a show but I know she's afraid. I can hear it in her voice, a tremor, a wave in her voice on the phone. Like her voice is water and there is something roiling underneath.

They used to reassure me she was doin' FINE. They'd call me all the time and say how much they *cared* about her, how well she was doin' and I stupidly believed them. Now they *don't* tell me anything. Because, can you believe it? She's in a federal penitentiary now. I have no idea why they moved her there, she's absolutely terrified. "I'm in here with killers, Mom," she said to me. She even smashed a TV to get put back into segregation, because she's so afraid.

Now they *can't* tell me anything. Because she's over eighteen. Because of the confidentiality, can you believe that . . . And she won't tell me. Because she doesn't want to worry me. That's the kind of thoughtful child she is.

But I do worry, because they have a sickness when it comes to my Glory. But they always have had—even in juvenile detention, they used to tease her without mercy—callin' her Princess because she did have the nicer things—and putting a silly crown on her . . . Though she did have some very good friends there, and she was heartbroken to leave . . . you see it's like she had finally found her people, her tribe, right? But the guards . . . they just . . . I don't know, it's as if she somehow got this reputation, and right across the country in all those institutions they treated her according to the reputation, instead of the sweet girl right in front of them. I mean, she was so sweet, the mum's in federal, when she was in the population—would have her watch their babies! Oh Glory loved children . . .

I am just hoping . . . hoping against hope, that those guards have enough humanity, to know . . . that coming home is all that girl needs . . . that they would let her raise her voice, or even spit or yell and just . . .

Let her be.

So we can walk hand in hand around Pleasant Point and she can finally feel the fresh air on her cheek.

I am her mother and I don't need them to tell me something is not right.

My cousins, they have a dairy farm near here and although they are very nice people, they do treat their animals good, when I look at the calves in those . . . pens, the veal pens . . . they are chained inside those cramped, shiny, blinding white, and it makes them so nervous they are insane, you can't pet them—Whenever I think of Glory, I think of those calves.

I won't eat veal now— Veal is young, you can taste how young it is, sweet and tender.

That is my Glory. They have put her in the veal pen.

GLORY #2

GLORY is in her cell, looking at the crocodile she sees coming up through the cell floor. There is a camera in the corner of room.

...... My mother . . . is a crocodile. Not my mother mother, SHE is an angel down in Nova Scotia, but my . . . birth mother, my . . . crocodile mother. Oh I know 'cause I can feel her eyes on me, those tiny green eyes hard on me, lookin' right through me to my bones—shakin' my bones, and waiting.

She is in the swamp the swamp you don't see and I don't see but I feel . . . right under me, moving, wet, and waiting. Can you smell it? I can smell it now, all the time. Smells like dead mice and dog food. But sometimes like a baking cake. Really good and really bad. And I feel her . . . waiting and I say to her no. No I am not yours to have I am mine and I am not I am not going to be sucked under the mud by your crocodile eyes so stop lookin' at me.

You . . . can't have me.

(to the camera) And you can't have me you fuckin' crazy ugly faced perverts you can't fuckin' touch me without my consent. I'm reporting you I'm reporting you to God and my crocodile and I'm telling you she is gonna open her big big mouth and her teeth is gonna stab through your head and she is gonna chew you up into tiny little pieces and feed you to her OTHER babies hey wanna wrestle? I could wrestle ya come on in here and . . .

Sound of guards entering.

No, Gail, come on, I was only foolin' around, I didn't mean it.

Come on, you know I was only . . . No. No . . .

> GLORY *moves as if she has been spun around to face the wall.*

Stop fucking squeezing my neck. Stop fuckin' squeezing my neck—you're hurting me!! You're hurtin' my . . . I can't fuckin' breathe . . .

> GLORY *is in a straitjacket and head restraint, sometimes called "the wrap." She cannot move.*

Think of something nice, that nice nurse Cindy in Saskatoon said think of something nice when they put you in this fuckin' wrap and this . . . helmet so your head can't even move, when they do this to ya, just daydream, your dreams'll keep ya goin', your dreams my dreams my dreams . . . my . . . oh yah, yah . . .

The bus goin' to the war museum in Ottawa and it was winter and so much snow but it had melted and then frozen up so it was like a fairyland outside the windows, and so the whole grade nine and ten is goin' and we are all packed in the bus but no one it sittin' beside me, but I like my own company and I'm imagining about the story of the Snow Queen, and how I could be her, like, waving a giant icicle and ah freezing everyone I don't like—turn 'em into statues. Ice statues that wouldn't never melt unless I said . . .

. . . and then HE gets on the bus later, eh, 'cause he lives in the country and he looks around and he stands there for a second and then . . . sits beside me.

And I am like oh my god 'cause he was so hot, right? My heart's pounding I swear everyone could hear it pound—he was in grade ten and his name was Ravi and he was like a hockey star.

And I'm thinkin': well he's prolly just sittin' beside me 'cause there is no where else to SIT, then he's like:

"How're you doin' there, appleface?"

Ahh—do I say "fine" or "not bad" or "I'm good" or "how are you?" or "do I really look like an apple?" I don't KNOW.

And I am like losin' it like an earthquake inside my guts and I smile and say "good," and he takes my one ear bud and puts it in his actual ear and listens! And we're listening . . . to my music . . . together . . .

And he smiled. At me.

And then its getting dark 'cause it's a long long way and we are drivin' over this bridge and he takes my face in his hands . . .

He kisses me. And it's like my whole body was melting chocolate spreadin' over something . . .

Okay don't lie, Glory, he didn't kiss you but he did listen to my music with me he did do that and they can't ever take that away—

(to the camera) You can put me in chains and this crazy wrap and this fuckin' hockey helmet you can take my pillow you can take my blanket so I'm fucking freezing all the time you can take my paper and crayons and my Harry Potter and you can even take my mind but you can't take my memories.

You can't take my memories.

GAIL #2

(to an imaginary group of VIP visitors) Welcome, welcome to Grand Valley. Oh yeah, it is a cold one, cold for April, eh? Well it'll warm up soon enough. Always does!!

So my name is Gail, and I have the distinct honour of showin' youse all around the facility.

Grand Valley, or GVI, as we call it, ya might say is almost a model women's prison! It's organized around these quite nice cottages as you can see, and the women live five or six to a cottage and they can cook and clean together, like co-operate, help each other out. . . and yet, if they want they have their own rooms— so they do have their privacy too.

Oh, something else we are quite proud of: According to a 2005 annual report by HM Chief Inspector of Prisons for England and Wales, and I quote: "Grand Valley is a relatively open and healthy prison, fostering safety, respect, purposeful activity, and reintegration."

It's not perfect, it's not ideal, and we keep working to be better . . . but as prisons go, it's pretty good."

Now GAIL *addresses the audience.*

Pretty impressive, eh? Yah, that there is the party line. And if you never looked in segregation or TQ—that's "therapeutic quiet"—you might even think its true. And the fact is, that when I showed those bigwigs around last week, Kim Pate from Elizabeth Fry was there and she asked them come on and have a look at the girls in segregation, she . . . implored them actually, and though the loyal-employee part of me thought no way it's none of their business they don't understand what they're lookin' at, the other part of me, the real part of me thought yeah. Go in. See what conditions . . . see what that kid Glory has to . . . and we . . . we are forced to be part of what is happening to her. So that part of me, the deep-down part, was very disappointed when they all declined.

I wanted them to see . . . what we have to cope with.

Down there every working day . . .

Like . . .

We are not just security guards.

Like someone who stands in front of your condo, lets you in and out. We are not goons with keys.

You need training for this.

You need college training. Gun training. CPR, serious training in the rules, the protocol of a penitentiary.

You see, legally, you don't even have to touch me for me to charge you with assault. You just have to look like ya might, and have the ability to do so—

And therefore an inmate can be charged and should be charged for . . . behaving in a threatening kind of way, I mean if I feel threatened by you, if you are raisin' your hand to me or even your voice I will charge you so fast it'll make your head spin. Some of 'em have seven, eight hundred charges and they deserve every one. Others, like Glory, well, she does deserve some of them, I have laid 'em on her myself, but—I don't know. Confidentially, the other day, she put her hand through the meal slot and Andy ups and charges her, and that's another sixty days. And half of me thinks all those charges might be why she started that crazy choking of herself before. Thank Christ she hasn't done it in a while.

But when she was choking herself before, we hadda be so careful when we went in, right?

Right? Like if I go in and stop her from hurting herself, like, I grab her hand, I might well be charged with assault myself—others have been. I'm telling you, with these rules of theirs? They got us tied up tight and fuckin' gasping for breath.

GLORY #3

See I figure: she was gliding around in the swamp one day and and she saw this handsome fisherman on the shore, he was fishin' for carp and she like JOLTS outta the water to eat him but what he did bein' a really quick thinker and prepared for anything, is he dove inside her mouth and through her body and out the other end, but he left something there he left his sperm! And so so the sperm swam up into the crocodile egg and then a half-human, half-crocodile embryo grew and grew and grew and grew and grew and one day the crocodile mother she crawled up on land and she laid this giant big egg but had to go back into the swamp and luckily, a nice big red hen came along and sat on it to keep it warm and then when it was spring and the tulips were blooming and people were dancing guess what. The egg c-c-c-c-c-c-cracked, I remember, I remember the feelin' of bein' in that egg and just wanting to just dance out see I pushed and pressed and . . .

And there was a hand . . . and over there was a foot, and an eye and—

GLORY was BORN.

Listen. I am not crazy—even though they frequently inject me with meds for schizophrenics, which is totally fuckin' ILLEGAL I know I wasn't, um, born of a crocodile really.

But I am FEELING . . . her, I am feeling—

I feeeeel her.

Her crocodile eyes behind my eyes.

The scaly skin behind my skin.

I can feel her knife-sharp teeth in my mouth.

And her GIANT tail inside me. Flapping when I am pissed off at Gail, making me do bad things.

The crocodile part of me ramming ramming against the girl part of me.

Just tryin' to get out.

To get me back to the swamp.

Where she wants me so I can't go home to my mom and Ravi.

And ohhh she wants me bad. Badder and badder every day.

"But I'm not goin' back to you, mother crocodile, so don't wait up for me!"

I'm getting out of here one day.

And I'm headin' home . . . to go to the mall with my friends, party at night, get drunk, and finally get a boyfriend.

I plan to get kissed, dude.

So you can just sink right back into your smelly swamp!

ROSELLEN #2

A lady never speaks harshly. A lady never uses curse words.

Especially *the F-word*. Good Lord!

A lady never expresses a controversial opinion that might upset people.

A lady never, ever shouts. In fact, never raises her voice.

Do not fidget do not touch your hair do not put your hands in your pocket do not rock back and forth never ever look in the mirror in a restaurant. All of that. That's the way we all were, except you know, those girls. The girls that went into the barn with the boys and lost their reputations. The girls that had babies at fifteen, and went on the welfare and nobody respected them or their child again.

Except me. Oh I respect them. I am sure it was not easy for them and we have no right to judge them, none at all. And in fact, I am grateful to a girl like that. Because if it wasn't for a girl like that goin' into the barn and getting herself into trouble, I would not have been given my Glory.

Oh yes, I am still grateful . . . that she is my daughter, and I always will be . . . and I say to my mother and all her lady lessons, to hell with being a lady—nobody LISTENS to ladies . . .

I've got to start raisin' my voice—I've got to shout for those bureaucrat robots to even hear me; in fact, I will have to howl like a wounded animal to get my daughter home.

GLORY #4

Renee, next cell to mine?

She's my best friend in the whole world.

We talk through the walls.

And we make up stories.

And poetry to keep each other goin'.

To keep each other sane.

Renee?

She is havin' the worst day of her life.

She got declared a dangerous offender. Which means she won't ever get out.

I mean Renee . . .

She never hurt nobody.

Alls she did is

1. Be Indian.

2. Try to escape, can you blame her?

And 3. Take hostages.

Okay, that sounds serious but I KNOW Renee, and she would never have hurt nobody.

She just wanted them to see how desperate she was.

She wanted them to LISTEN.

They said in the report that she and the other one tied up and tortured the guards for three hours.

It wasn't like that I know, because like I tol' ya we talk through the walls.

They did tie them up, but only because they needed them to listen. They did NOT torture them not at all. Okay, one little burn with a cigarette but that was only because the guard called her a stupid Indian. Look. Renee needed to see her children, she has four children she couldn't never see, and one of 'em was sick with leukemia . . . she somehow thought that they would let her see her children when she let the guard go, it's all those bad movies, I coulda told her, you're wastin' your time, girlfriend. This is not gonna end well for nobody.

That woman loves her children more than life itself and all that happened is she got twenty-one more years.

> GLORY *knocks on the cell wall.*

Renee?

Hey, Renee!

I got one for ya. It's time for my Monday poem. Are you listening? Can you hear?

So I am the girl
In your storybook swirl
On Friday I was in a fiery car wreck
and the EMS saved me
So now I wear
this lovely green ribbon round my neck,
but sometimes I bleed through
and the EMS becomes PMS.
Get it? Get it, Renee? EMS and PMS?

So that's my Monday poem, Renee.

You have Tuesday! Hey. Sleep well, eh.

I'm prayin' for your Samantha, you know I am. They got good
medications for cancer these days, I heard that.

I love you too. I like really love you.

GAIL #3

Some of them love the life inside.

They'll say they hate it. But they like it.

Some of them will commit a crime the day they get out.

So they can come back in.

They are comfortable here.

They know where they stand.

They know who they are.

They have a place.

On the outside, they're the people beggin' for change.

Gimme a loonie gimme a toonie—

Gimme five bucks for food. Sellin' their bodies . . . for drugs.

I can recognize them instantly, even if I don't know them. It's something in the face, in the body.

The way they hold themselves.

This place stains them.

Forever. All of them.

It stains some of US too . . .

And the thing of it is . . . it's an unwipeoffable stain . . .

GLORY #5

You wanna hear something like crazy? So this morning, I am butt-naked in the shower, and they get it in their heads that I am holding some kind of weapon.

They all pile in with their hockey helmets and that and I tell them, "Leave me alone, I want my privacy," but they keep after me, *(into megaphone)* "Give us the knife." "It's not a knife, it's only a tampon, I'm on my period," I tell 'em. "Give it here," they say, "you could hang yourself with that, give it to us." "No," I say, "I'm not givin' you, I'm bleeding I need it," and they go, "Glory, we are gonna pepper spray you if you don't give us that item immediately," and I am like, "Do it, dudes! Go right ahead and blind me if it'll make you feel better."

So that's what they did. They blinded me. For like thirty minutes, and it fucking hurt, I couldn't see nothing.

I still can't really see.

Did you know pepper spray is from hot peppers? Like the ones they put in Mexican food?

Ever been pepper sprayed? One time they pepper sprayed me nine times in one day.

"Give a little, get a little," that's what Gail kept saying, what does that mean?

Give a little, get a little. I just don't fuckin' get that, do you?

ROSELLEN #3

I know people judge me. I know they're thinking, "What kind of mother would turn out a daughter like that." I know they are imagining TERRIBLE things went on in my house behind closed doors.

And I know that in most cases, a girl acting out like Glory did? That might be the case. But I can assure you, it is NOT.

When Glory came at five-days-old I thought I finally know what ... JOY is, deep, resounding joy. God, if you like.

To me, Glory is an angel. Because I know that she came straight from the arms of God.

I did everything by the book; she had love, she had limits. She had healthy food and dancing class and storytime every night. She watched *Sesame Street*, and *Dora the Explorer*, and some of the Disney movies but not anything violent. I invited her little schoolmates to our home ...

There was ... nothing ... to predict ... what would happen.

They haven't let me visit her, hardly at all for this last YEAR. Well, they keep movin' her around—seventeen times in the last year—three times I have bought and paid for plane tickets only to be informed that she was no longer at that institution. And do you think they pay me back? Hah!

Her letters—oh I used to get her letters every day and they used to bring me such joy and also break my heart, because she tried to be so upbeat. With the little smiley faces, and hearts ... But now, I don't get them at all. Since they took away her paper and her pencils. Don't ask me why ... when all that girl was living for was writing her poetry and making her drawings and her beautiful stories.

I can't see her, so just have to go on trust, now. Trust that she is ... doin' okay ... trust that they are not ... harming ... her ... trust ...

Is worthless. I do not have any trust in the system whatsoever my trust is like cigarette ash in my mouth.

Ash. In my mouth.

GLORY #6

So I know you tol' me to stop talkin' but, Gail, I have to tell you I have to tell you what is happening here in my TQ cell, that when it's real real quiet like late late at night, I start to hear this sound, this scratching sound and then I see a cockroach or two but the cockroach starts to grow, and turns green and gets bigger and bigger till she's like nine feet long and with tiny green eyes and she's a crocodile, and she is in the swamp like my floor, Gail, turns into a SWAMP, right? And she and her friends are swimming around and the thing is, that she is my mother my real mother crocodile because the truth is that I am part-crocodile, Gail, I know you want me to stop talkin' but the thing is that I can't, I try to stop and my mouth just keeps on goin' because when I stop talkin', Gail, I start to disappear . . .

Gail, it's been four hours. I tol' ya I fuckin' pissed myself.

One time Gail asked me, "How come you never cry?" and I realized she was right. I stopped crying when I was about fifteen, when I had been in prison for over a year. I wanted to cry, even just to make them feel sorry for me, but I couldn't. I can't.

GAIL #4

Incessant chatter and talking. Oh, can that girl talk! I've had her charged six times for that. She won't shut up. She keeps . . . telling me that she's not human. That she's part . . .

Crocodile. Really, you know? Glory is eighteen, going on twelve.

She keeps referring to the swamp. It's part of her . . .

Mentalness.

Her . . . disordered thinking. She screams at me—

"I got seventy-five teeth and I will tear you to pieces."

She says, "I am two hundred million–years–old, Gail, how old are you?"

She has imagination, I will give her that. She says the wildest things.

But all the crazies do, you know. They can talk, right? They use words in a way I wouldn'a thought of.

And I'll tell you something else most people don't know.

Over half of them in here?

Are lunatics.

I mean straight-out, hearing-devil-voices, seeing-pink-ele-phants—

Totally crazy. And they don't get treatment. Are you kidding me?

They see a shrink for five minutes, maybe once.

MAYBE once. And all that psychiatrist does is prescribe some worse-than-useless pill that has them drooling and shitting their pants.

'Course, this whole place would make anyone crazy, right?

Like the rules, the rules are . . .

Like. I know and every other CO knows that they will suitcase glass shards or whatever—means they store tiny pieces of glass or whatever they can up their body cavities so they can use them for makin' whatever later and the fact is we can't search them without their consent. And you think they're gonna give their consent? We know as soon as we turn our heads or change shifts or whatever they could be makin' ligatures or even knives with their toothbrushes. And there's not a damn thing we can do.

This whole place is fucking crazy. Like the world turned upside down.

ROSELLEN #4

Twenty-nine days.

I can hardly say it out loud. I am afraid I will jinx it.

In official mail. After five years of hell—my Glory is comin' home.

I read it over every day, every morning, soon as I open my eyes.

She will be coming home in time for spring.

In time for daffodils and tulips and then later on in the summer my morning glories.

In time for shorts and sittin' on patios havin' ice cream and riding her bike, oh she loved to ride her bike she used to ride it all around the neighbourhood.

That's what I'm telling you, she was just an ordinary kid, oh yes! Never wanted to be away from Mom, drove in the front seat with me all the time till her playin' around with the radio made me crazy and I sent her to the back seat.

Well when she comes home . . . she can play with the radio as much as she wants.

Unless she gets another charge. On the phone I begged her I said—

Glory, you must be the perfect inmate, now think of all the things we are gonna do, we will go hiking round the Cabot Trail, drive down the South Shore to Lunenburg, swim in the ocean . . .

And she promised, oh she promised she wants to come more than anything else in the world so I know she will be good. And—

Years from now this will all be a bad dream. We will look back at this terrible time and shake our heads. Glory will be—I don't know, a hockey coach or a teacher or a mum with seven beautiful, happy kids running around and we will be sittin' right here in this kitchen playin' cards and we'll see something on the TV about a prison and we will look at each other just shake our heads. It'll be like yes it happened? But it never happened. That's what it'll be like.

GLORY #7

I wonder if bein' tasered jumbles up your brains. Ravi won't like me if I've gone stupid. When they were transferring me from Joliette to the private airplane they got for me they tasered the shit outta me. I was like "please don't taser me—I'm not gonna DO anything, come on! I'm scared!"

And they point that thing at me and they—

BZZZZZZZZZZZZZZZZZZZZZZZZZZZZZ

> *GLORY relives the tasering.*

It's like bein' fuckin' killed. They tasered me twice in New Brunswick and that is totally illegal. Your brain gets shattered like glass into a thousand pieces all over the floor, and I been tryin' to sweep 'em up and glue 'em back together ever since. I still am . . . for Ravi, and for my mom. 'Cause guess what? Fuck you, mother crocodile . . . WHOOO! I'm goin' home.

ROSELLEN #5

Every child born . . .

Is born to all of us.

We are ALL responsible—

We are ALL responsible.

These things go on.

That's what I have come to understand.

All around us . . . in the . . . wings . . .

In the dark.

In the shadows . . .

We don't even know they are there.

Till they affect us in some way, and we are pushed to the shadows and . . .

We see . . .

What goes on.

And we are astonished . . .

You know, ever since I found out Glory will be comin' home?

I have been wondering about her biological mother.

I sometimes wonder if she senses what happened to Glory.

One day . . . when all this is behind us.

One day I plan to . . . to locate her.

To meet her for coffee and to . . .

Tell her the truth.

My heart is just racing.

It started racing after the crabapples.

And it has not slowed down.

Since.

Ever been swimming the day after a storm?

Glory and I always loved to swim in the ocean! And oh we will be doin' that again when she comes home. Every summer weekend!

I was on the synchronized swim team in college, so to improve our strength we would go to the Bay of Fundy and swim. And I was an excellent swimmer, I was, so one time, everyone else had left, but I wanted to swim some more, so I was walking on the shore, lookin' for a good spot to go in, when I suddenly noticed the tide rushing in, fast, faster than you can imagine. The Bay of Fundy has the highest tides in the world! And there is ocean on one side, and forty foot cliffs on the other. And I start to run, scrambling over the rocks, and the tide is covering my feet and then my knees and by the time I got to the other side it was up at my neck.

> ROSELLEN *crosses towards centre stage, along* GAIL*'s hallway.*

There is not an hour goes by where I don't imagine . . .

That I am in that segregation cell.

Inside my daughter.

I see the white walls.

I see the white floor.

The camera.

The little window, the evil eyes looking at me.

I am wearing the shift that she wears.

I am cold.

I know she is cold.

GLORY #8

Hey, Gail, how are you today? You are looking pretty no I mean it, well pretty for an old lady only kiddin', will ya loan me your glasses? Just for a minute? I'm goin' home so I'm practising to be an actress, 'cause I'm goin' on TV for real. Come on, you don't need 'em, I'll give 'em back, I just need to practise for a minute. Nobody won't give me nothing. I promise I won't hurt them. Please. *(to GLORY's surprise, GAIL passes her glasses through the meal slot)* WHOAAA!!! Thank you.

>   GLORY *grabs the glasses, plays with them.*

GAIL #5

>   *A recording plays. We hear GAIL and GLORY with the cell door between them.*

Come on, give 'em over, give 'em back to me, Glory, right now. I'm goin' on break and I need them to read the paper.

Glory, give 'em now. This is a direct order, Glory, do not be foolin' around with those glasses, so help me God I need them to see—right now, come on . . .

Glory, will you give me back my glasses now.

Glory dear, I need those glasses back now . . . I know you can hear me. Just put them through the meal slot.

This is a direct order—

Glory, so help me God give me those glasses now—

GLORY #9

I'm sorry, Gail. I really really did not mean to break them. I was just . . . playin', like if they were my friend Serena's from juvie because she had glasses just like this and we were best friends we used to read Harry Potter to each other through the walls and and so I was like putting the glasses on and being her, and whippin' them off and being me and . . . I'm sorry, Gail. Don't report me. Please? Please. Because if you report me—

GAIL #6

Those glasses cost me four hundred dollars. I had to report her because that's the only way I can get the money back. With the forms filled out. Of course that means another charge, but I had no choice. I had to report her.

She's always had a thing for my glasses. And I know I shouldn'a given in, but I was kinda feelin' sorry for her and I figured she couldn't really do any damage with a pair of glasses . . . though I knew it was against the rules to give her ANYTHING I thought . . . fuck the rules . . . But I shoulda known better than to feel sorry for the girl. The girl is a criminal.

You can't fool around with these people. There have been riots; prison riots, in which COs are captured and killed.

You have to understand the criminal mind.

One thing you can never be?

Is a friend.

And if you think you can?

You are out of your mind.

You will find out soon enough.

That these people are NOT your friends.

That most of 'em?

Would kill you as soon as look at you.

They will give you a long, warm hug and stab you in the back so that knife is comin' out your belly. And they will laugh while they are doin' it.

Listen: four hundred dollars is two weeks of groceries.

ROSELLEN #6

They say they are not.

Letting her come home.

They are not letting her out when they said they would.

Sixty more days.

Ashes in my mouth.

She is impossible, they said.

She has another assault charge

For taking a COs glasses and breaking them.

She is not getting out for at least another sixty days . . .

She is impossible.

I ask you; who wouldn't be impossible?

When they are treated like a monster.

Oh god—

When I imagine . . .

My baby in what do they call it?

The "wrap."

I want to kill them.

I am sorry. I am a woman of peace.

I would not hurt a housefly.

But when I see them in my mind putting a goalie's mask on my daughter's beautiful face.

I see her hands and her legs wrapped and restrained.

And I hear her crying for help.

I ask God for superpowers.

I ask God: GOD, let me grow wings in the night.

Wings of steel-cutter blades.

Let me fly to the GRAND VALLEY torture chamber,

And cut my way through.

Flying at the speed of Superman . . .

To my daughter.

To rip off the wrap.

To crack open the mask, the shackles.

To put my baby . . .

On my back and fly.

GLORY #10

It's my crocodile mother. Can you hear her? I can hear her call me. Like . . . a siren, as loud as a siren and I am feelin' her eyes just arrowing into me and her tail inside me again and her skin in my skin and her mouth . . . on my head on my neck pullin' pullin' me back down *(GLORY drops to the ground and begins to slither on her stomach)* into the swamp right here right underneath me she is thinking into my thoughts she is thinking it's sweet in the swamp, baby girl, it's so sweet and muddy and thick and smells like bakin' cake you can glide through the swamp you can crocodile yourself as far away down the swamp as you . . . thick and smellin' sweet like wood fire and honey cake and all those crocodiles, bringin' me home . . .

> *GLORY takes a strip of cloth from her pocket and tears it to make a ligature, then ties it and puts it around her neck. She walks in circles, her breathing laboured, and then faints.*
>
> *A recording plays. GAIL's tone is measured but increasingly distressed.*

"Glory, take that thing off your neck. I am not playing your game. Take that off. That's a direct order. She's blue. We're going in."

GAIL #7

GAIL stands, holding the ligature.

I think it's disgusting. Most of us do. We talk amongst ourselves and we are so pissed off, we know it's wrong. Now that she is back to tyin' the ligature round her neck five times a day . . . But you know, that's the way she was anyway . . . The warden is like, "She's just doin' it to get attention, and the more you go in the more she will do it, so you're not goin' in." "You're not goin' in," she says, "till Glory stops breathing." Till she is blue.

Well when someone isn't breathing, what are they, eh? When someone isn't breathing, they are fucking dead. When you stop breathing, you are friggin' blue and you are dead, aren't you? Isn't that what living is? Breathing? When we have gone in like that, when she's going blue and we breathe into her or whatever what we are doin' is bringing her back from the dead. And I did not sign up for that.

GLORY #11

They do not know the loneliness here.

They do not know the feeling of having no one to look at, to talk to, no one to touch.

The feeling of being the only person in the whole world.

If I could get a pair of socks . . .

A nice pair of clean socks . . . I could shove them down my throat.

I hope it's raining when I die. I like that idea, of me being on the floor, my face purple, my body eaten by crocodiles, my bones— cold as the floor . . . and the rain just pouring down.

ROSELLEN #7

Ever been to a bullfight? My ex-husband and I went on holiday to Spain and . . . when I think of that.

I imagine her: that young calf, in the veal pen, now grown into a bull:

A bull in the ring with all the coloured spears sticking out of her body, still fighting, still moving, and the crowd cheers and laughs, and claps, and the bullfighter . . . the matador stabs her again . . . and she slowly loses strength, and her spirit, and that is what scares me to death: I sense her spirit has been . . . drained out of her . . .

GLORY #12

GLORY writes with her finger on the wall, her own secret message, the same poem as before. With the ligature, GLORY hangs herself. Over the sound of the death rattle, the guards recorded voices are heard.

GAIL #8

"Glory? Do you need us to come in and take that off you? Glory, you sit up right now."

"Glory, come on, we have work to do. Come on, knock it off, we have work to do."

"Glory, come on, wake up, sit up so Frank can come take that off you. And don't try anything."

"If you bite him, so help me God."

"She's not responding."

The sound of the cell door opening.

"Slap her."

The sound of a slap.

"Come on, Glory, we have work to do."

"Come on, knock it off, we have work to do. Come on, Glory."

"Oh my GOD. I think she's dead."

"Holy fuck, I haven't had fuckin' CPR in eleven years."

"Call the medics."

"Call the fuckin' medics."

"Glory? 1—2—3."

"Fuck."

"At approximately 8:10 a.m. in her TQ cell on October 26, 2007, at Grand Valley Institution for Women, in the presence of myself and six other correctional officers, the prisoner asphyxiated herself with a ligature."

ROSELLEN #8

I will never forget the morning I brought you home, a summer morning, so all the morning glories were blooming, and the vine on our porch had flowers so blue, such a beautiful blue there really are no words for it and THAT was the colour of your eyes.

My morning Glory . . .

GAIL #9

I do not appreciate having that video all over the Internet. I have a right to my privacy. I have a right to go out with my children and not be harassed and insulted by people who know nothing of what they are talking about.

My rights have been violated.

Do any of you work? Do any of you understand this? We could not afford to lose our jobs . . .

"Criminal negligence causing death"? Are you kidding me?

That is like calling us murderers.

Murderers for doing our jobs.

WE HAD OUR ORDERS.

Do NOT, do NOT go in until she has ceased breathing.

Time enough to save her life.

But not time enough for her to enjoy it.

Once she is breathing. Out you go. Tough love.

Teach her and teach her good. We didn't like it. That's what they ordered us to do.

Somebody spread it around that we were laughin'.

While she was choking to death.

That one of us said, "Aren't you dead yet?"

I know I am going to be fired.

And then what the hell will I do?

WHAT will I do with my life?

Be a crossing guard?

> GAIL *steps into* GLORY's *cell.*

They call that hypoxic.

'Cause it means there is no oxygen getting to the face.

The veins are . . . blocked by the ligature.

Her face . . . was like that moment.

When dusk . . .

Turns to dark.

Pitch black. No life.

ROSELLEN #9

Oh, I know.

I know what you would say to me.

What you are sayin' to my avenging angels. The jury.

The investigators.

You were just doing your job.

That's what they keep saying at the inquest. They had their orders, it was very hard for them, she was acting up.

My daughter did NOT want to die.

She wanted to live.

She tied ligatures around her neck . . .

Because . . . she . . . had faith.

She had faith that they cared enough about her.

That her country cared enough about one of its daughters.

That those guards would have to save her.

So she needed her life saved many times a day.

So she would know that it was worth living.

She wanted to live.

ROSELLEN *shows a small quilt covered with signatures.*

Isn't it beautiful? The kids at Saint-Jérôme . . . the juvenile detention centre where they called her Princess? They made it for her. And they all signed it. Look: "To a sweet angel—now you have your wings." They really loved Glory there . . . she would be right chuffed to see this. I am going to get it framed, like, in a show box . . . so everyone can see . . . how loved she was . . .

ROSELLEN *steps into* GLORY'S *prison cell.*

I went to see that prison. With the reporter.

Grand Valley. Can you imagine, giving a place like that a name like that?

It reminds me of how they had musicians playing classical music when people came into the concentration camps.

Grand Valley. I see that sign, this building. I see death.

This was her death place. Really, that is what it was.

You are gone. You are . . . ash.

But, Glory . . .

I know you can hear me.

I know you can hear my every thought.

And I know, they know . . .

You are watching.

END

© Guntar Kravis

Judith Thompson is a two-time winner of the Governor General's Literary Award for *White Biting Dog* and *The Other Side of the Dark*. In 2006 she was invested as an Officer in the Order of Canada and in 2008 she became the first Canadian to be awarded the prestigious Susan Smith Blackburn Prize for her play *Palace of the End*. Judith is a professor of drama at the University of Guelph and lives in Toronto.

First edition: October 2016

Printed and bound in Canada by Imprimerie Gauvin,
Gatineau

Cover art by W. R. Moore Illustration

**PLAYWRIGHTS
CANADA PRESS**

202-269 Richmond St. W.
Toronto, ON
M5V 1X1

416.703.0013
info@playwrightscanada.com
playwrightscanada.com

A **bundled** eBook edition is available
with the purchase of this print book.

CLEARLY PRINT YOUR NAME ABOVE IN UPPER CASE

Instructions to claim your eBook edition:
1. Download the BitLit app for Android or iOS
2. Write your name in **UPPER CASE** above
3. Use the BitLit app to submit a photo
4. Download your eBook to any device

MIX
Paper from
responsible sources
FSC® C100212